Aditya Kumar

Cryptography and Chaos a New Approach in Network Security

Aditya Kumar

Cryptography and Chaos a New Approach in Network Security

LAP LAMBERT Academic Publishing

Impressum / Imprint
Bibliografische Information der Deutschen Nationalbibliothek: Die Deutsche Nationalbibliothek verzeichnet diese Publikation in der Deutschen Nationalbibliografie; detaillierte bibliografische Daten sind im Internet über http://dnb.d-nb.de abrufbar.
Alle in diesem Buch genannten Marken und Produktnamen unterliegen warenzeichen-, marken- oder patentrechtlichem Schutz bzw. sind Warenzeichen oder eingetragene Warenzeichen der jeweiligen Inhaber. Die Wiedergabe von Marken, Produktnamen, Gebrauchsnamen, Handelsnamen, Warenbezeichnungen u.s.w. in diesem Werk berechtigt auch ohne besondere Kennzeichnung nicht zu der Annahme, dass solche Namen im Sinne der Warenzeichen- und Markenschutzgesetzgebung als frei zu betrachten wären und daher von jedermann benutzt werden dürften.

Bibliographic information published by the Deutsche Nationalbibliothek: The Deutsche Nationalbibliothek lists this publication in the Deutsche Nationalbibliografie; detailed bibliographic data are available in the Internet at http://dnb.d-nb.de.
Any brand names and product names mentioned in this book are subject to trademark, brand or patent protection and are trademarks or registered trademarks of their respective holders. The use of brand names, product names, common names, trade names, product descriptions etc. even without a particular marking in this work is in no way to be construed to mean that such names may be regarded as unrestricted in respect of trademark and brand protection legislation and could thus be used by anyone.

Coverbild / Cover image: www.ingimage.com

Verlag / Publisher:
LAP LAMBERT Academic Publishing
ist ein Imprint der / is a trademark of
OmniScriptum GmbH & Co. KG
Heinrich-Böcking-Str. 6-8, 66121 Saarbrücken, Deutschland / Germany
Email: info@lap-publishing.com

Herstellung: siehe letzte Seite /
Printed at: see last page
ISBN: 978-3-659-68363-3

Dedicated to my parents

Abstract

The main objective of this thesis is to present chaos based Multi message signcryption schemes with public verifiability. This thesis represents two publicly verifiable chaos based signcryption schemes:

1. Multi Message Single Recipient Signcryption Scheme
2. Multi Message Single Recipient Signcryption Scheme

Chaos and cryptography have some common features, the most important being sensitivity to initial conditions, parameters' and variables' changes. To achieve high security, purposed scheme uses a Multi Chaotic Key Generator (MCKG) to generate multiple keys for signcryption scheme. Both the schemes are publicly verifiable, highly sensitive to the initial conditions, and provides high security due to chaotic keys used in encryption and decryption schemes. Being publicly verifiable signifies that digital signature of the sender can be verified by any trusted third party without the knowledge of receiver's or sender's private key.

Keywords: *Signcryption, chebyshev polynomial, hash function, keyed hash function, encryption, decryption, digital signature,*

Acronyms

AES	Advance Encryption Standard
CA	Certificate Authority
CPK-MM-MR-SS	Chaotic Public Key multi-Message Multi-Recipients Signcryption Scheme
DES	Data Encryption Standard
DSS	Digital Signature Standard
KH	Keyed Hash Function
MAC	Message Authentication Code
MD	Message Digest
OWHF	One Way Hash Function
PK-MMS	Public Key Multi-Message Signcryption
RSA	Rivest Shamir Adleman
SDSS	Shortened Digital Signature Scheme
SHA	Secure Hash Algorithm
TTP	Trusted Third Party

Notations and Symbols

/	Divide
*	Multiplication
$\|\|$	Concatenation
=	Equality
$\equiv$	Congruence
$E_k(.)$	Symmetric key encryption
$D_k(.)$	Symmetric key decryption
G	Group
$\|x\|$	number of bits in x
$hash(.)$ or $H(.)$	one way hash function
mod	Modular operation
Z_P	set of non-negative integers less than p
$\varphi(m)$	Euler's totient
$\oplus$	XOR operation
$\wedge$	AND operation
$\vee$	OR operation

Table of Contents

List of Figures

List of Tables

Chapter 1
Introduction

Information, in most restricted technical manner, is a series of symbols that is interpreted as a message. Information, kind of event, affects the states of a dynamic system. Conceptually, information is a message (word or expression) that is being conveyed. The idea of information is closely related to notions of representation, constraint, data, pattern, communication, knowledge, understanding, instruction, form, mental stimuli, meaning, control, perception, and entropy. Moreover, information is a kind of assent and like other assent it also has a value. Information is valuable because it affects an outcome, behavior or a decision. Therefore, information needs to be secured from attacks.

The modern era has been well-developed and tremendously advanced. Security has become an essence in almost all areas of communication. Cryptography is the study of mathematical techniques related to aspects of information security, such as privacy or confidentially, entity authentication and data integrity. While sending a message over an insecure channel such as internet we must provide security features such as confidentiality, integrity, authenticity and non-repudiation [1]. These are the four major security goals of cryptography [2].

Before the modern era of cryptography, it was exclusively concerned with the confidentiality of information (i.e. encryption and decryption) - conversion of messages from a comprehensible form to an incomprehensible one and back again, making unreadable by interceptors or eavesdroppers without secret knowledge (namely the key needed to decrypt the message). In recent decades, cryptography was intended to ensure secrecy in communications, such as those of spies, military and diplomats. The field has now expanded beyond confidentiality concerns to comprise techniques for message integrity checking, digital signatures, sender-recipient authentication and interactive proofs and secure computation among others. In ancient times, the use of cryptography was limited to a small community forms by the military and intelligence agencies. The keys were distributed secretly between sender and receiver by a courier and the same key is used to encrypt and decrypt the message.

Encryption technology for civilian use is a fairly new development. Many major historical developments released to the public only in retrospect, after being known, but kept classified by the military authorities. A rare exception is revolutionary article by Claude E. Shannon, "Communication Theory of Secrecy Systems" [3], published in 1949.Shannon applied field machinery he created himself, information theory, to the problem of private communication. The article presents ideas, such as redundancy and entropy, which are of great importance for future research. It gave a solid mathematical theory basis for the cryptography.

In 1976, Whitfield Diffie and Martin Hellman introduced the concept of public-key cryptography [4], although it was known to both American and British intelligence for some years. In short, the public key encryption is the Kerckhoffs principle which is taken to its logical extreme. Instead of requiring secret key for encryption and decryption, only the key used for decryption must be secret. The sole idea behind public key cryptography is a one way mathematical function. For such a function g, it is easy to compute $g(x)$ for a given x, while computing x from given $g(x)$ is hard. The idea behind this is that a user picks some x as his private key, and publishes $g(x)$ as his public key. A cryptographic operation is then performed over a message m using $g(x)$; in such a way that x is needed to reverse it. This also opens doors for digital signatures, as sender can use his knowledge of x to perform cryptographic operations over a message m whose correctness can then be verified using $g(x)$.Another important influence Diffie and Hellman found together with the public specification of the Data Encryption Standard (DES) in 1975, and the RSA in 1977 which led to the birth of cryptography as a research field in academics [5].

A problem with public key cryptography, however, is that it is slower than symmetric key cryptography. It requires more processing cycles to both encrypt and decrypt the contents of the message. To provide authenticity of the message, i.e. the proof of originator, the sender needs to sign the message before sending it to the recipient. To achieve authenticity, the sender uses any one of the digital signature schemes [6, 7] depending upon security desired. In a typical communication system the communication channel is considered to be insecure. Confidentiality, integrity and non-repudiation are the most necessary features of cryptographic system. To achieve these goals, in traditional approaches, the information is digitally signed and then encrypted before transmitting over an unsecure network. The sender signs the message using digital signature algorithm and then encrypts the message (and the signature) using a private key encryption algorithm under an encryption key, chosen randomly. The randomly chosen encryption key is then encrypted using the recipient's public key. This two-step approach is called "signature then encryption".

Until 1997, message digital signature and encryption have been seen as essential but distinct building blocks [8, 9] of numerous cryptographic schemes. Encryption and signature generation consumes machine cycles, and also introduce "expanded" bits to the original message. In 1997, Y. Zheng combines both the operations logically in a single step, called Signcryption [1]. The idea behind Zheng's scheme is to perform signature and encryption in a single logical step with a cost significantly lower than required by the traditional signature-then-encryption approach.

1.1 Digital signature

A digital signature is a mathematics scheme, demonstrates the authenticity of digital message or document. Valid digital signatures provide a recipient reason to believe that the message is created by a acknowledged sender and it has not changed in transit. Digital signatures are widely used for software financial transactions, distribution, and there where it is important to detect forgery or tampering. Below are some common reasons for applying a digital signature to communications:

- **Authentication:** it verifies **who you are**. Although the messages may often include information about the entity sending the message, the information may not be correct. Source can be authenticated using a digital signature of the message.

3

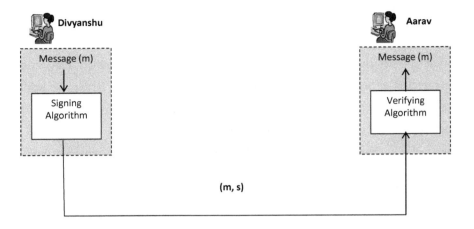

Figure 1.1: Digital Signature Process

- **Integrity:** The recipient should have the ability to verify that the received message is the original one, sent by the sender
- **Non-repudiation:** by this property, an entity which has signed some information cannot deny later having signed it.

Figure 1.1 below shows the digital signature [10, 11] process. Here Divyakshi and Aarav are sender and receiver, respectively. Divyakshi uses a digital signature algorithm to sign the message. Divyakshi sends message and signature to Aarav. Aarav applies the verifying algorithm and verifies the Divyakshi's signature over received message. Many digital signature schemes have evolved over the past decades. Some of them have been applied [12]. They are: *ElGamal digital signature scheme, RSA digital signature scheme, elliptical curve digital signature scheme, Digital Signature Standard (DSS), Schnorr digital signature scheme.*

1.2   Encryption

Encryption stands for conversion of messages from a comprehensible form into an incomprehensible one and back again, rendering it unreadable by eavesdroppers or interceptors without secret knowledge. The data processing steps required for the transformation of the plain message into cipher text is called message *encryption*, and

4

the reverse procedural i.e. recovering original message from cipher text is called *decryption*. Various parameters are used by an encryption algorithm, are derived from a secret key. As discussed previously, we have a variety of encryption algorithms, which can broadly be divided into two categories: *Private or Symmetric key algorithm* and *Public or Asymmetric key algorithms* [6, 7]. DES or AES are Symmetric key message encryption, whereas RSA is an asymmetric key encryption algorithm. Now we can apply both operations (signature and encryption) one after another to provide confidentiality and authenticity. This is known as "Signature-Then-Encryption" approach [1]. This approach is discussed in detail in the next section.

1.3   Signature-then-Encryption

In order to send a confidential message in a way that it cannot be forged, it's been a common tradition for a sender to sign it first and then put it in an envelope, seal it before handing it over to be delivered. Discovery of public key cryptography has made communication possible between people, who have never met before, over an open and insecure network such as Internet [13], in a secure and authenticated way. Before sending a message the sender needs to do the following:

1. Sign the message under a digital signature scheme (DSS)
2. Encrypt the signature and the plain message using a symmetric encryption algorithm under randomly chosen symmetric key
3. Encrypt the symmetric encryption key using receiver's public key
4. Send the encrypted message to the receiver.

This approach is known as Signature-then-Encryption and is shown in the Figure 1.2 (a) and Figure 1.2 (b).

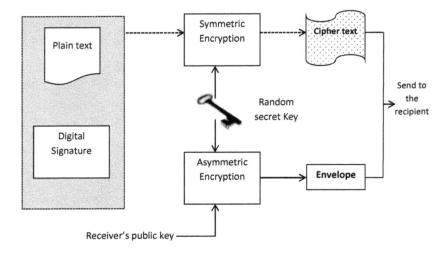

Figure 1.2 (a): Signature-then-Encryption (Sender side)

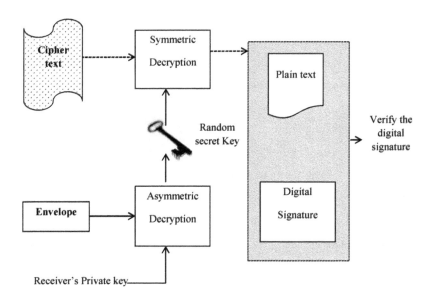

Figure 1.2 (b): Signature-then-Encryption (Receiver side)

1.4   Drawbacks of Signature-then-encryption scheme

The main drawback of this approach is that, digitally signing a message and then encrypting it, needs more computational power and consumes more machine cycles and also bloats the message by introducing extended bits into it [1]. Hence, decrypting and verifying the message at the receiver's side, a lot of computational power is used. Thus we can say that the cost of delivering a message in authenticated and secure way using signing-then-encryption is infect the sum of the costs of both digital signatures and encryption.

Now a question rises, *"whether it is possible to send a message of arbitrary length in authenticated and secure way with a cost less than that required by signature-then-encryption."*

This problem never seems to be solved since the invention of public key cryptography. In 1997 Y. Zheng [1], introduced new cryptographic primitive called "signcryption" which meets both digital signatures and public-key cryptography in logic one step, and with a cost significantly less than that required by signatures then encryption. It is discussed in next section and in chapter 2 in detail.

1.5   Signcryption

Signcryption scheme was first introduced by Y. Zheng in 1997 in his article *"Digital Signcryption or How to Achieve Cost (Signature & Encryption) << Cost (Signature) + Cost (Encryption)"* [1]. In his article Zheng asks whether one can perform authenticated and secure message transmission over unsecured network more efficiently than by composition, and proceeds to give a positive answer, by devising a new scheme that provides both services while saving computations cost and bandwidth, called *"Signcryption"*. Signcryption is a new paradigm in public key cryptography that simultaneously fulfills two functionalities digital signature and public key encryption in a logically one step, and with a cost significantly lower than that required by "signature then encryption" approach. Today, signcryption is an active research area and a significant amount of research is being carried out in this field. Since 1997, many signcryption schemes have been proposed [14, 15, 16, 17 and 18]. Signcryption is discussed in detail in chapter 2.

1.6 Thesis Organization

This thesis is structured as follow. In 2nd chapter signcryption is discussed in detail. Discovery of signcryption, basic signcryption algorithm, improvements over signature than encryption schemes and applications of signcryption is discussed here. Various literature surveys are discussed in chapter 3. H. Elkamchouchi chaos based scheme and H. Elkamchouchi, M. Emarah and A. A. Hagras scheme are discussed in detail.

In chapter 4 chaos theory and mathematical background of cryptography is discussed and illustrated in detail. Chebyshev polynomial is also discussed and properties of chebyshev polynomial are discussed here in this chapter.

In chapter 5, two signcryption scheme based on chaos are purposed which works in single messages and multi messages environments. The security features and cost saving are analyzed. This chapter also includes the snapshots of implemented scheme.

Finally, in chapter 6 concluding remarks, limitation of work and future scope are discussed.

Chapter 2
Signcryption

2.1 Introduction

The word signcryption was first invented by Yuliang Zheng in 1997 at Monash University, Australia. According to him signcryption [1] is a cryptographic primitive which accomplishes both the purposes of digital signature and public key encryption logically in a single step, and with a computational cost significantly lower than that of traditional signature-then-encryption approach.

2.2 Discovery of Signcryption

2.2.1 ElGamal Public Key Encryption and Signature

The specific version of ElGamal public key encryption and digital signatures [19], Yuliang was interested in involved three parameters that were public to all:

1. p: a large prime number.

2. q: a prime factor of p−1.

3. g: an integer in the range of [1,...,p−1] with order q mod p.

Consider two users Divyakshi and Aarav. Divyakshi has a private key x_a chosen randomly from [1,...,q−1]. She sets her public key $y_a = g^{xa} \bmod p$. Likewise, Aarav's private key is an integer x_b chosen randomly from [1,...,q−1] and he sets his public key as $y_b = g^{xb} \bmod p$.

Now assume that Divyakshi wants to send a message m to Aarav securely. Divyakshi first needs to look up Aarav's public key y_b in a public key directory. Divyakshi then picks up a random integer x from [1,...,q−1]and calculates $w = y_b^x \bmod p$.

This is followed by employing an appropriate one-way hash algorithm hash to calculate a key from w called an encryption key $k = hash(w)$ for a suitable private key cipher (E, D) where E is encryption scheme and D is a decryption scheme. Finally Divyakshi sends to Aarav the following pair of data items as a cipher text of m:

$$\text{ElGamal Encryption: } (c1, c2) = (g^x \bmod p, E_k(m))$$

Upon receiving (c1, c2), Aarav can recover key k by calculating $k = hash\ (c_1^{xb} \bmod p)$. He can then use the decryption algorithm D and k to decrypt c2 and obtain m.

Divyakshi's signature on a message m is composed of two numbers (r, s) which are defined as

$$\text{ElGamal Signature: } (r, s) = (g^x \bmod p, (hash\ (m) - x_a \cdot r)/x \bmod (p-1))$$

Aarav and any other third party can verify the authenticity of Divyakshi's signature on the message by using her public key y_a. Looking closely at the ElGamal encryption and signature algorithms, one can notice that both algorithms contain the following item:

$$g^x \bmod p$$

This quantity can be viewed as playing the role of an "ephemeral key" in both algorithms. A question, which rises here, is *"whether it is possible to let the same "ephemeral key" serve as a channel linking the encryption and signature algorithms together."*

There are numerous tweaks of and improvements to the original ElGamal signature. The most notable ones include Digital Signature Standard (DSS) or Digital Signature Algorithm (DSA) [20] and the Schnorr signature [21]. These two signature techniques are defined as

$$\text{DSS: } (r,\ s) = ((g^x \bmod p) \bmod q, (hash(m) + x_a \cdot r)/x \bmod q)$$

$$\text{Schnorr: } (r, s) = (hash(g^x \bmod p, m), (x - x_a \cdot r) \bmod q)$$

Two more interesting variants are obtained by further shortening variants of theDSS. These two shortened versions are called SDSS1 and SDSS2 and are definedas

$$\text{SDSS1: } (r, s) = (hash(g^x \bmod p, m), x/(r + x_a) \bmod q)$$

$$\text{SDSS2: } (r, s) = (hash(g^x \bmod p, m), x/(1 + x_a \cdot r) \bmod q)$$

Here, one can notice that $g^x \bmod p$ does not explicitly appear in any of the variants of the ElGamal signature discussed above. Nevertheless the quantity can be easily derived from these signatures by a signature verifier. All these four variants show a significantly shorter signature size than that of original ElGamal signature. This brings up another interesting question i.e. *whether it is possible to combine ElGamal signature and encryption in such a way that the results do not contain $g^x \bmod p$.*

After a number of trials and errors, in 1997 Y. Zheng came up with a very nice combination of ElGamal signature and encryption called *"signcryption"* that answered both of the questions asked above.

2.3 Preliminaries on signcryption

A signcryption scheme typically consists of three algorithms: *Key Generation, signcryption, Unsigncryption*. The key generation algorithm generates the public keys required for signcryption phase and unsigncryption phase. It also generates the key pairs of Divyakshi and Aarav. The signcryption scheme will generate signcrypted text (c, r, s) and send it to Aarav. Aarav, the recipient decrypts the message and checks the authenticity of the message in the unsigncryption phase using public key of Divyakshi.

A signcryption scheme should have the following properties: [22]

A. *Correctness*: Any signcryption scheme should be correctly verifiable i.e. signcrypted text formed by signcryption algorithm must be accepted by the unsigncryption algorithm.

B. *Efficiency*: Computational costs and communication costs of signcryption scheme should be less than those best known traditional signature then encryption schemes with the same provided functionality.

C. *Security*: A signcryption scheme should simultaneously fulfil the security attributes such as:

a) *Confidentiality*: It should be computationally infeasible for an attacker to observe any partial information of a signcrypted text, without knowledge of the sender's or designated recipient's private key.

11

b) *Unforgeability*: It should be computationally infeasible for an attacker to masquerade a sender to create an authentic signcrypted text that can be accepted by an unsigncryption algorithm.

c) *Non-repudiation*: The recipient should be able to prove to a third party that the sender has sent the signcrypted text. This ensures that the sender cannot deny his signcrypted texts.

d) *Integrity*: The recipient should have the ability to verify that the received message is the original one, sent by the sender.

e) *Public verifiability*: Any third-party without any practice on the private key of the sender or the recipient can verify that the signcrypted text message is a valid signcryption of its corresponding message.

2.4   Working of Signcryption

A signcryption scheme typically consists of three algorithms: *Key Generation, signcryption, Unsigncryption*. The sender *Divyakshi* uses the public key of the receiver for generating the secret key in the signcryption phase and uses her private key to sign the messages and then sends the signcrypted text (c, r, s) to receiver Aarav. After receiving the cipher text and the digital signature, Aarav uses his private key to recover the same secret key and using that key he decrypts the message and recognizes the authenticity of the message originator [13]. Algorithms of signcryption scheme are discussed in the next sections.

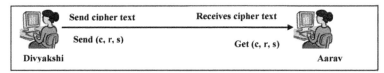

Figure 2.1: Alice sends cipher text (c, r, s) to Bob

2.4.1 Key Generation Phase

Different phases of signcryption scheme are discussed here after. These include: key generation phase, signcryption phase and unsigncryption phase. In key generation, public parameters are defined along with parameters key pairs of sender and receiver are generated. The public parameters used in the process of signcryption phase and unsigncryption phase are given below:

Public Parameters:

- p: a large prime number
- q: a prime factor of $p - 1$
- g: a integer with order $q \bmod p$ in $[1 \dots p - 1]$
- *hash(.) or H(.)*: a one way hash function.
- KH : a keyed one way hash function.
- $E_k(.) / D_k(.)$: symmetric encryption/decryption algorithm with private key k such as *AES or DES*.

The private and public keys of sender and receiver are generated in the following manner.

Sender's key pair:

Pair of sender's key (x_a, y_a) is computed as follow:

x_a: Sender's private keychosen randomly from $[1, \dots, q - 1]$

y_a: Sender's public key computed as:$y_a = g^{x_a} \bmod p$

Receiver's key pair:

Pair of receiver's keys (x_b, y_b) is computed as follow:

x_b: Receiver's private keychosen randomly from$[1, \dots, q - 1]$

y_b: Receiver's public key computed as:$y_b = g^{x_b} \bmod p$

2.4.2 Signcryption phase

In this phase, Divyakshi the sender computes the signcrypted text. To perform signcryption she needs receiver's (Aarav's) public key y_b and computes a master key k. further she splits k in k1 and k2 of same length. Now, encryption of plain text is done using k_1 and $k_2$is used to compute keyed hash value using a keyed hash function.

At last Divyakshi signs the message using her private key x_b. The algorithm of signcryption phase is as follow:

Sender side:

1. Choose x uniformly at random from $[1,...,q-1]$,

   and compute $k=hash(y^{xb} \bmod p)$.

   Split k into k_1 and k_2 of appropriate length.

2. Compute $c = E_{k1}(m)$.

3. Compute $r = KH_{k2}(m)$.

4. Compute $s = x/(r + x_a) \bmod q$.

5. Output (c, r, s) as the signcrypted text to be sent to Aarav.

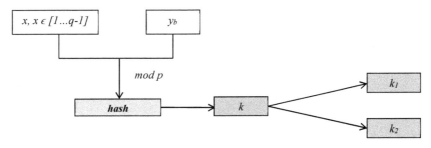

Figure 2.2: Key generation for signcryption

Figure 2.2, shows the key generation process for signcryption phase. Generated key k is splited into to sub keys k_1 and k_2.

Figure 2.3 below, shows the signcryption phase, where message m is encrypted under k_1 and reyed hash value is generated under k_2

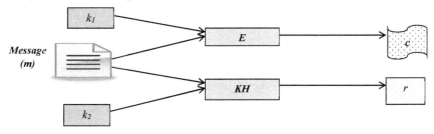

Figure 2.3: Signcryption phase

Figure 2.4 below, shows the signature process. Signature over a message is generated using r (computed previously) and sender's private key x_a.

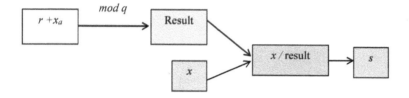

Figure 2.4: Signature process

2.4.3 Unsigncryption phase

In this phase, Aarav the Receiver first recovers master key k using his private key x_b and sender's public key y_a. Further he splits k in k_1 and k_2 of same length. Now, decryption of cipher text is done using k_1 and k_2 is used to compute keyed hash value using a keyed hash function and verifies the authenticity of the message. Unsigncryption algorithm is s follow:

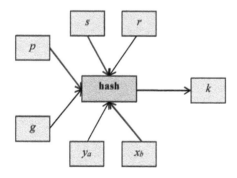

Figure 2.5: Recovering master key k on receiver's side

Receiver's side

1. Recover k using s, r, g, p, y_a and x_b as
   $k = hash((y_a \cdot g^r)^{s \cdot xb} \bmod p)$.
2. Split k into k_1 and k_2.
3. Recover plain text m $=D_{k1}(c)$.
4. Accept m if $KH_{k2} = r$ this ensures that the sender of the message is Divyakshi. Reject otherwise.

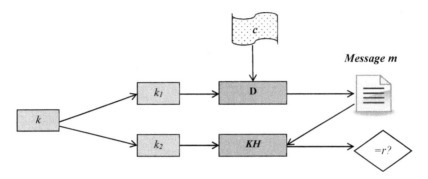

Figure 2.6: Decryption and Verification on receiver's side

Figure 2.5 shows the needed parameters to recover the master key on the receiver's side as calculate in the step 1 of unsigncryption phase. After recovering the key k receiver splits it into k_1 and k_2. Now using the symmetric key decryption algorithm D under k_1 receiver recovers the plain text and verifies the authenticity of message as shown in figure 2.6.

The original signcryption algorithm required a few tweaks in order for its security to be proved with mathematical rigor [9, 23]. The modified algorithm employs two separate one-way hash algorithms U and V. The former was used to generate a key for a private key cipher whereas the latter to compute the value of r. In addition, both Divyakshi's public key and Aarav's public key participated in the hash computation of r, whereby the cipher text was tightly bound to both Divyakshi and Aarav, preventing possible abuse by dishonest Divyakshi or Aarav.

2.5   Advantages of Signcryption

The advantage of signcryption scheme over signature-then-encryption schemes [1] lies in the dramatic reduction of communication overhead and computational cost which can be symbolized by the following inequality:

Cost (signcryption) ≪ Cost (signature) + Cost (encryption)

To compare the efficiency of two different methods for secure and authenticated message delivery, two types of cost involved [1, 13, and 24]: *computational cost* and *communication overhead* (also known as storage overhead).

2.5.1 Saving in computational overhead

The *computational cost* indicates how much computational effort has to be made both by the sender and recipient of messages. Generally, the computational cost of an algorithm is estimated by counting the number of leading operations involved in computation. Typically these operations include symmetric key encryption and decryption, modular addition, hashing, division, multiplication and exponentiation. Along with computational cost, digital signature and encryption based on asymmetric key cryptography also require extra bits to be added into a message. This is known as *communicational overhead*. On the basis of these two cost parameters, we can say one algorithm is better than another if these costs are less in the former algorithm as compare to the later one.

Yuliang Zheng in [1] gives the comparative analysis of signcryption scheme, which was based on DLP, with signature-then-encryption schemes. From this comparison, it is clear that signcryption scheme saves computational time as well as communication overhead as compare to other traditional schemes.

With the signature-then-encryption based on Schnorr digital signature and ElGamal encryption [7], the number of modular exponentiation is three, for both the processes. Out of three, two of them are used for verification of the signature. That is why they spent more time in computing $g^s.y_a^r \bmod p$, where p is a large prime number. For faster calculation of the product of multiple exponentials with the same modulo, Shamir [13] suggested a new technique (see Appendix A), on an average in (1+3/4) |q| modular multiplication, where q is a prime factor of p.

As, a modular exponentiation can be done, on average, in approximately 1.5|q| modular multiplications by the well-known square-and-multiply method [4], (1+3/4) |q| modular multiplication is computationally equivalent to 1.17 modular exponentiation.

Thus, the number of modular exponentiations involved in the decryption-then-verification process of Schnorr digital signature scheme, can be reduced from 3 to 2.17. Combined computational cost for both sender and receiver will be 5.17 as compare to 2.17 for the Zheng's signcryption scheme. Therefore, we can calculate the total percent of saving as follow:

$$(5.17 - 2.17)/5.17 = 58\%$$

So this represents a reduction of 58% in average computational cost.

2.5.2 Saving in communication overhead

In signcryption, the saving in communication overhead will be,

$$\frac{|hash(.)| + |q| + |p| - (|KH(.)| + |q|)}{|hash(.)| + |p| + |q|}$$

Yuliang Zheng assumed that $|hash()| = |KH()| \approx |q|/2$. If $|p| = 10240$ bits and $|q| = 320$ and $|hash()| = 160$ bits. Hence the saving in communication overhead will be 96%.

2.6   Applications of signcryption

In many applications, both confidentiality and authenticity are needed together. Such applications include secure email (S/MIME), web browsing etc. In order to achieve these two goals (confidentiality and authenticity), many cryptographic schemes have been made: Schnorr signature-then-ElGamal encryption, DSS-then-ElGamal encryption, RSA signature-then-RSA encryption, Schnorr signature-then-RSA encryption, RSA signature-then-ElGamal encryption.

As discussed above, signcryption is a more efficient method for secure and authenticated message transfer, so it can be applied in many applications include secure email, web browsing, digital payment systems and many more. If we could apply digital signcryption in this area, then we could save 50% computational cost and up to 96% communication overhead.

Chapter 3
Literature Review

3.1   Introduction

Many of the proposed signcryption schemes include modular exponentiation while some of them are based on elliptic curves. Y. Zheng [1] proposed signcryption scheme in 1997 which saves about 58% computational cost and upto 96% communication cost than that of traditional signature-then-encryption scheme. This scheme was based on DLP (Discrete Logarithmic Problem). It involves modular exponentiation and RSA that takes a large key size of about 1024 bits. After that, Jung et al. showed that Zheng's scheme does not provide forward secrecy of message confidentiality if the private key of sender is disclosed. They also proposed a new signcryption scheme based upon discrete logarithm problem (DLP) with forward secrecy.

In Jung's scheme [25], even if attacker is able to obtain the sender's private key, he cannot find the corresponding original message yet that sender has sent. However, in those research results, when a disagreement occurs, the judge cannot directly verify the signature without the knowledge of recipient's private key. Bao and Deng [26]enhanced Zheng's signcryption scheme such that the judge can verify signature without the prior knowledge of recipient's private key, but a key exchange protocol is required for process of verification. Gamages et al. [27] modified Zheng's signcryption scheme in a way anyone can verify the signature of cipher text. Their scheme only verifies the cipher text to maintain confidentiality of message in firewall applications.

Chen-huang WU, Zhi-xiong Chen purposed a new certificate less Signcryption scheme which is more efficient than the only certificateless signcryption scheme previously proposed by M. Barbosa and P. Farshim in "Certificateless signcryption", Proceedings of the 2008 ACM symposium on Information, computer and communications security. A new character *"public verifiability"* is introduced, into certificate less signcryption scheme. This scheme can also be extended to scheme can easily be extended into a multiple-receivers scheme [28].

Abdel-Aty M. Emarah, Hassan M. Elkamchouchi and Esam A. A. Hagras jointly developed an efficient public key multi-message signcryption (PK-MMS) scheme for secure communications. This scheme is based on the intractability of Discrete Logarithm Problem (DLP) and used a multi-key generator to simultaneously signcrypt multiple messages. The main purposeof the proposed scheme is to design multi-key generator that generates keys for the block cipher and keyed hash algorithms. The proposed scheme is compared with Zheng signcryption scheme which costs 50% and 75% less in computation cost for two and four signcrypted message than that of Zheng's signcryption scheme. The main drawback of this scheme is that it does not provide public verifiability [29]. An improvement to the scheme was introduced in [30]. This new approach was based on the intractability of three hard problems: DLP (Discrete Logarithm Problem), DHP (Diffie-Hellman Problem) and OWHF (reversing a One-Way Hash Function). This scheme is publicly verifiable and uses MKGR (Multi Key Generator Routine). However, this scheme is efficient and publicly verifiable, still uses extra cycles in computing keys for Keyed hash function. Algorithm of this scheme is discussed in detail in section 3.2.2.

However, signcryption schemes purposed earlier do not provide public verifiability. Later, various signcryption schemes with public verifiability have also been purposed [28, 30, and 31]. Rapid development in computational power of today's systems increases the demand of highly secure communication systems. Most of the research work at present on symmetric key cryptography focuses on block based algorithms in which blocks of messages are subjected to numerous rounds of computation with the help of a single or multiple keys. Such algorithms are mainly based on the DES algorithm which bears a 56-bit key on 64-bit blocks with 16 rounds of key dependent computation.

With current computational resources available a hacker can try each of the 256 keys possible in the DES algorithm and thus crack the encrypted message. It is therefore no longer secure to use a single key to encrypt all data. The obvious solution is to use multiple keys, a different key for encrypting each block of data. But this has practical limitations, as all the multiple sets of keys have to be maintained at both the sending and the receiving ends which make the work harder. Also the number of multiple keys unless extremely large in number will not pose any challenge to the hacker who we assume has unlimited resources at his disposal. Another solution to this is to generate one-time pads for encryption with the help of a single key and various chaining algorithms. But since encryption algorithms are publicly known, the above procedure critically depends on the security of the single key. The idea of using one time pads or mathematical functions for generating multiple keys has been largely unexplored.

However, simple mathematical functions are not sufficient for this. It is always assumed that the encryption algorithm is public which means that the function to generate the multiple keys is known to the hacker as well. This means that once the hacker is able to find one key, he immediately has access to all other keys. This is where chaotic functions can play a major role. During the last years, the study of chaotic system and its possible applications to Cryptography has received considerable attention in a part of the scientific community. Like Dr. Ranjan Bose [32] explored an algorithm using the chaotic function $f(x) = p*x*(1-x)$ to generate multiple keys for symmetric key cryptography. The encryption steps proposed in the algorithm consist of a simple XOR operation which should be sufficient unless there is a known cipher text or plaintext attack. But if this attack is said to be consider, this operation will no longer provide secure encryption. Also various complex chaos functions like Lorentz equations, Well Oscillator equations or other fractal equations can be applied to generate multiple keys. Algorithm of this scheme is discussed in detail in section 3.2.2.

3.2 Chaotic theory for signcryption

Current cryptographic techniques are based on number theoretic or algebraic concepts. Chaos is another paradigm, which seems promising. A large number of applications in real systems, both natural and man-made, are being investigated using this novel. Cryptography and chaos have some common features, the most prominent being sensitivity to parameters' and variables' changes. Therefore chaos based cryptosystems have many useful and practical applications in security field. Like Dalia. H. Elkamchouchi [33] proposed scheme makes use of the chaotic system implemented at the transmitter receiver end as a chaotic multi key generator producing n chaotic keys to be used by the proposed scheme. This scheme presents important improvement over the "Public Key Multi-Message Multi- Recipient Signcryption" (PK-MM-MRS) scheme which was published before. Use of a chaotic message mixer at the transmitter receiver end to obtain maximum security.

Zheng [19] introduced a single message signcryption for multiple recipients where a message is broadcasted through a channel so called multicast channel; one of whose properties is that all recipients will receive an identical copy of a broadcast message. Major concerns with broadcast to multiple recipients include security, unforgeability, non-repudiation and consistency of a message. A new chaotic public key multi-message multi-recipients signcryption scheme [33] has removed these issues. But the major issue with this scheme is the use of simple function which when performed the circular Right shift operation on the original key give rise to multiple keys is not said to be secure. This scheme is not publicly verifiable also, which is one of the most desirable property of public key cryptography.

3.3 Related work

3.3.1 H. Elkamchouchi chose based signcryption scheme

This scheme[33] uses a chaos based multi key generator which is based upon chaotic behavior of $1/\pi$. This scheme uses a CMM (Chaotic Message Mixer) which adds the multi-message signals (m_1, m_2, ... m_n) to the output of the chaotic map in the chaotic message mixer which in turns produces the chaotic mixed multi message (m_1', m_2', ..., m_n').

The main drawback of this above scheme is that it doesn't provide public verifiability which is one of the most desirable feature of public key cryptography. And no significant research has been carried out on chaos based signcryption schemes. Next section describes H. Elkamchouchi et al. scheme which provides public verifiability. However this scheme is not chaos based but it also uses a multi key generator.

3.3.2 H. Elkamchouchi, Mohammed Nasr and R. Ismail signcryption scheme

This scheme [30] is an improvement over [29]. It uses a multi keys generator routine (MKGR) to generate multiple keys. This scheme uses a shared-secret key computed using Diffie-Hellman key exchange algorithm.

However, this scheme provides public verifiability but if we analyze it closely we find that to generate publicly verifiable signature keyed hash value is generated using k_i which are the outputs from MKGR. Here, master key k is publicly recoverable, so there is no need to parse the master key k into MKGR.

3.4 Observation

So finally it has been observed that out of all signcryption schemes H. Elkamchouchi's scheme is based on chaos but it does not provide public verifiability. It also uses cipher algorithms four times (for single message), two for encryption–decryption of symmetric master key and two for encryption–decryption of message which can be reduced. So our objective is to purpose a new signcryption scheme based on chaos which works for both single recipient and multi recipient, uses less number of cipher algorithms and provides public verifiability.

3.5 Problem Definition

Although several signcryption schemes have been proposed, some of them are proved to have security problems. H. Elkamchouchi's scheme is the only chaos based signcryption scheme. But this scheme does not provide public verifiability and also uses more number of cipher algorithms. Due to rapid development in communication technologies, there is a high demand of highly secured cryptographic techniques for secure communication. Cryptography and chaos [discussed in chapter 4] have some common features, the most prominent being sensitivity to parameters' and variables' changes. This can provide dynamic structure for key generator which in turns provides very high security. So we need to formulate signcryption scheme based on chaos with public verifiability.

3.6 Summary

Signcryption is a new cryptographic primitive which can fulfill both message encryption and signature logically in a single step thus reducing the computational cost and communication overhead. For the implementation of signcryption and unsigncryption algorithms, based on chaos, we must know about the chaos based cryptosystem and mathematics of cryptography. These are discussed in Chapter 4 in detail.

Chapter 4
Chaos Theory and Mathematical background of Cryptography

4.1 Chaos Theory

Chaotic functions were first studied in the 1960's and show numerous interesting properties. Chaos is one type of complex dynamic behavior generated by determined nonlinear dynamic systems. One of the soul parts of chaos theory is pretty easy to understand, though. It's often called the "*butterfly effect*". This can be understood in the following manner: a butterfly flapping its wings in China can have a huge effect on the San Francisco weather a few days or months later. That is, an infinitesimally little change at one point in a moment can make things totally unpredictable in the future. Figure 4.1 (a) and Figure 4.1 (b) show the butterfly effect in the Lorenz attractor [34].

This phenomenon can be modeled mathematically as follow:

$f(x)$ = fractional part of $10x$

That is, for instance, start with any number:

0.14285712981923460981485475125475

Multiply it by 10, and drop the whole-number part:

0.4285712981923460981485475125475

And again, getting:

0.285712981923460981485475125475

And so on. You can see that if there's a very tiny change in the original number, to:

0.14285712981923460981485475125474

Instead, after a certain number of iterations we'll have the HUGE change of 0.5 vs. 0.4 that was a 0.0000000000000000000000000000001% change or so is now a 20% difference after only 32 steps. Let's take an another example,

$f(x) = r*x*(1-x)$

26

Where *r* is a constant. If the constant r is 2.1, for instance, and initial value of *x* is 0.5, then after a few iterations we get 0.523809524. In fact no matter what the starting number is, function *f(x)* ends up at that number pretty fast, if r is 2.1. This is called an "*attractor*". It is like falling down a hill.

Now trying the same thing with r = 2.5 or 2.8 ...we approach different numbers (0.6, or 0.6428...), but still get closer to a single number. But if we start with r = 3.1, we find that the number heads after a little while towards a pattern where it bounces back and forth between two numbers like a pendulum: 0.55801412 and 0.76456652. And if we pick larger values of r, like 3.7, it seems to keep jumping around with no discernible pattern: this is called "*chaos*". And with the starting number of 0.5, after 50 steps you're at 0.921072984, but with the starting number of 0.50001, after 50 steps we are at 0.565549098, a completely different place. This is like the weather and this is called "*chaos*".

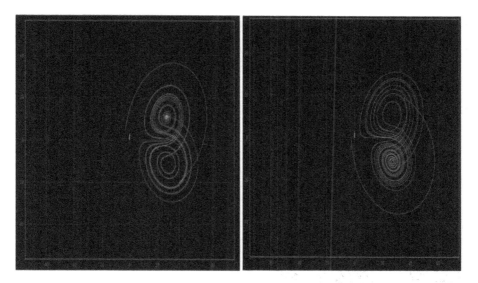

Figure 4.1: The Lorenz attractor, starting at two different initial points in x-coordinate.

In common usage, chaos means "a state of disorder". Small changes in initial conditions (such as rounding errors in numerical computation) yield huge diverging outcomes for such dynamical systems, rendering future prediction impossible in general.[35] This happens even if these systems are deterministic, i.e. their future behaviors are determined by their initial conditions and parameters, with no random elements involved[35]. Edward Lorenz summarized above as follows: [36]

Chaos: When the present determines the future, but the approximate present does not approximately determine the future.

Although there is no globally accepted mathematical definition of chaos, a commonly used definition of chaos stats that, for a dynamical system to be classified as chaotic system, it must have the following properties: [37]

1. Sensitivity to initial conditions,
2. Topologically mixing,
3. Dense periodic orbits.

However, it has been shown that the last two properties (Topologically mixing, Dense periodic orbits) actually imply first property sensitivity to initial conditions [39, 40]

4.1.1 Sensitivity to initial conditions

Sensitivity to initial conditions means that each point in chaotic a system is arbitrarily closely approximated by other point with significantly different future trajectories.

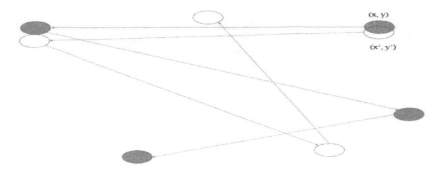

Figure 4.2: Sensitivity to initial condition

Thus, an arbitrarily small disturbance of the current trajectory leads to significantly different future behaviour. Figure 4.2 shows the value divergence for a chaotic map defined as follow:

$x \to 4*x*(1-x)$ and

$y \to x+y$ if $(x+y) <1$, otherwise $x+y-1$

The trajectories are as follow: (0.99434396, 0.67194495999999), (0.02249224209049338, 0.6943372020913932), (0.08794546454456206, 0.7823825566349552), (0.3208449085987445, 0.10332647623269985), (0.8714123810885389, 0.9748388523223487), and (0.9929599211932922, 0.6743085092293922), (0.02796206238821837, 0.7022705743174206), (0.10872074937271463, 0.8109913236801253), (0.38760219231420033, 0.19859351580332572), (0.9494669312298675, 0.1480605569341933).

4.1.2 Topologically mixing

Topological *transitivity or Topological mixing* means that the system will evolve over time so that any open set or given region of its phase space will eventually overlap to any other given region. This mathematical concept of "mixing" corresponds to the standard intuition, and the mixing of colored fluids or dyes is an example of a chaotic system.

A form of mixing may be defined, only using the topology of the system. A continuous map $f:x \to x$ is said to be **topologically mixing** if, for every pair of non-empty open sets A, B ϵ X, there is an integer n such that $f^n(A) \cap B \neq \varnothing$

Where f^n is the n'th iterate of f and a system is said to be **topologically mixing** if, for given open sets A and B, there exists an integer N, such that for all $n > N$, following is true: $f^n(A) \cap B \neq \varnothing$.

The chaotic map $x \to 4*x*(1-x)$ and $y \to x+y$ if $(x+y) <1$, otherwise $x+y-1$ also shows topologically mixing. In figure 4.3blue region shows transformation by the dynamics first to the purple region, after that to the pink and red regions. And eventually to a cloud of points, scattered over the space.

Figure 4.3: Topological mixing

4.1.3 Density of periodic orbit

Density of periodic orbit signifies that every point in the space is approached arbitrarily nearly by periodic orbits [46]. One of the simplest system, one-dimensional logistic map defined as $x \rightarrow a*x* (1 - x)$ is a systems with density of periodic orbits. For example, for a = 4, $\frac{5-\sqrt{5}}{8} \rightarrow \frac{5+\sqrt{5}}{8} \rightarrow \frac{5-\sqrt{5}}{8}$ is an unstable orbit of period 2 for the given logistic map. Similarly there exit orbit for periods for 4, 8, 16 etc. [44]. Bifurcation diagram for the logistic map is shown in figure 4.4 in which horizontal axis is the *r* parameter and vertical axis is the *x* parameter.

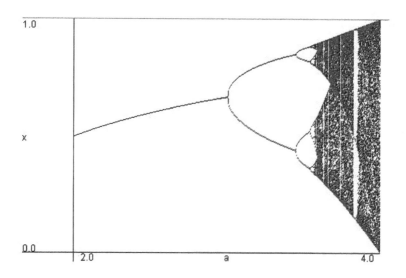

Figure 4.4: Logistic map bifurcation diagram

4.2 Chebyshev Polynomials

Chebyshev polynomials arise as the solution to the Chebyshev differential equation:

$$(1 - x^2)\frac{d^2y}{dx^2} + x\frac{dy}{dx} + n^2y = 0$$

For $n = 0,1,2,3.....$

Chebyshev equation is named after Pafnuty Chebyshev, a Russian mathematician.

let $x = cos\ t$, the differential equation then becomes:

$$(1 - cos^2t)\left(\frac{d^2y}{dt^2}\left(\frac{dt}{dx}\right)^2 + \frac{dy}{dt}\frac{d^2t}{dx^2}\right) - cos\ t\ \frac{dy}{dt}\frac{dt}{dx} + n^2y = 0$$

On solving, we get

$$\frac{d^2y}{dt^2} + n^2y = 0$$

whose solution is given by [46] :

$$y=Acos(nt)+Bsin(nt)\quad |x|<=1$$

$$y=Acos(narccos\ x)+bsin(n\ arccosx)$$

31

$$y=AT_n(x)+BU_n(x)$$

where $T_n(x)$ and $U_n(x)$ is known as the Chebyshev polynomial of the first kind and second kind respectively with degree n. Both polynomials are in the domain $[-1\ 1]$ and have their degree $n \in Z \cup \{0\}$. There are two kinds of Chebyshev polynomials but the first kind of polynomial is focused here.

The Chebyshev polynomial can also be generated using the following recurrence relation [45]:

$$T_{n+1} = 2xT_n(x) - T_{n-1}(x)$$

Where $T_0 = 1$, $T_1 = x$.

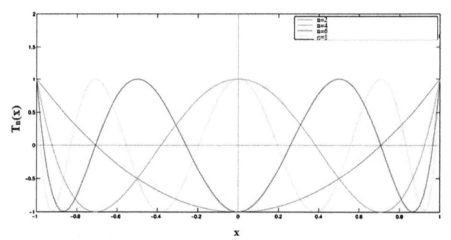

Figure 4.5: Comparison graph of first 4 even Chebyshev polynomials

First few even Chebyshev polynomials:

$T_0(x) = 1$

$T_2(x) = 2x^2 - 1$

$T_4(x) = 8x^4 - 8x^2 + 1$

$T_6(x) = 32x^6 - 48x^4 + 18x^2 - 1$

$T_8(x) = 128x^8 - 256x^6 + 160x^4 - 32x^2 + 1$

$T_{10}(x) = 512x^{10}-1280x^{8}+ 1120x^{6}-400x4+ 50x^{2}-1$

A very unique property of Chebyshev polynomial is that it is always restricted to the interval [-1 1] even if the degree of the polynomial is changed [47]. This is the property we are interested in and use in the purposed scheme. In Figure 4.5 a comparison graph among first 6 polynomials is drawn.

4.3 Mathematics of Cryptography

The basic properties of groups, rings, fields [2, 48, 49] are discussed in this Chapter along with extended Euclidian and Euler's theorem [2, 7].

4.3.1 Elementary algebraic structures

4.3.1.1 Groups

Definition 4.1: A Group (G) is a set of elements with a binary operator " $\cdot$ " that satisfies the following four properties:

a. *Closure*: If x and y are the elements of G, then $z = x{\cdot}y$ is also an element of G.

b. *Associativity*: If x, y and z are elements of G, then $(x \cdot y) \cdot z = x \cdot (y \cdot z)$.

c. *Existence of identity*: For all x in G, there exist an element e, called the identity element, such that $e \cdot a = a \cdot e = a$.

d. *Existence of inverse*: For each x in G, there exists an element x', called the inverse of x, such that $x{\cdot}x' = x'{\cdot}x = e$.

Along with those properties if it also satisfies the commutative property then it is called as *commutative group* or *abelian group*. Commutative property means for all x and y in G, we have $x \bullet y = y \bullet x$.

4.3.1.2 Ring

A Ring, is an abelian [7] structure with two operations + and $\cdot$ called *addition* and *multiplication*. For a given set R, ring maps every pair of elements of R to a unique

33

element of R. Both operations $(+, \cdot)$ must satisfy the following properties called **ring axioms** which must be true for all elements a, b, c in R:

- Addition is abelian [7], i.e:

  1. *Associative* under "+" operator: $(a + b) + c = a + (b + c)$
  2. There is an element 0 (**zero element**) in R such that $0 + a = a$
  3. *Commutative* under "+" operator $a + b = b + a$
  4. *element*: For each "a" in R there exists "$-a$" in R such that
     $a + (-a) = (-a) + a = 0$ ($-a$ is *inverse* of a)
  5. Multiplication $\cdot$ is associative:
     $$if\ (a{\cdot}b)\ {\cdot}c = a{\cdot}\ (b{\cdot}c)$$

- Multiplication distributes over addition:

  6. $a{\cdot}\ (b + c) = (a{\cdot}b) + (a{\cdot}c)$
  7. $(a + b)\ {\cdot}c = (a{\cdot}c) + (b{\cdot}c)$.

These seven axioms are all that are required for a set R to be a ring. A ring R satisfying the following property in addition:

  8. Multiplicative identity

There exists an element 1 in R such that $1\ {\cdot}a = a{\cdot}\ 1 = a$.

Although ring addition is commutative i.e. $a + b = b + a$. However, ring multiplication is not required to be commutative i.e. $a{\cdot}b$ needs not equal $b\ {\cdot}a$. Ring that also satisfies commutativity law for multiplication are called commutative rings.

4.3.1.3 Field

A field can be defined as follow:

A field is a commutative ring sometimes denoted by {F, +, *}, is a set of elements with two binary operations, called addition and multiplication. A set F (it can be numbers or other stuff) is called field if it satisfies the following properties:

1) Define on it "addition" according to these rules:

a) if a and b are the elements in F, then $a+b$ is also an element in F

b) if a, b, and c are the elements of F then $(a + b) + c = a + (b + c)$

34

c) if a and b are elements of F then $(a + b) = (b + a)$

d) there exists an element z in F so that for every element a in F, $a + z = z + a = a$

e) for each element a in F, there exists an element b in F so that $a + b = z$ and $b + a$ $= z$ (where z is the element introduced in 2d)

2) "multiplication" is defined on F according to these rules:

a) if a and b are elements of F, then $a*b$ is also an element of F

b) if a, b, and c are elements from F then $(a*b)*c = a*(b*c)$

c) if a and b are elements of F then $a*b = b*a$

d) there is an element n of F so that for each element in F, $n*a = a$ and $a*n = a$

e) for each non-zero element a in F, there exists an element b in F so that $b*a = n$
   and
   $a*b = n$ (where n is as described in 3d)

3) For all elements a, b and c from F,

$$a*(b + c) = (a*b) + (a*c) \text{ and}$$
$$(b+c)*a = (b*a) + (c*a)$$

F is then called a field under addition and multiplication. In essence, a field is a set in which one can do addition, subtraction, division and multiplication without leaving the set. Division is defined with the following equation:

$$a/b = a\ (b^{-1})$$

4.3.1.4   Finite Fields

Only finite fields are extensively used in cryptography. Galois showed that for a field to be finite field, the number of elements should be p^n, where n is a positive integer p is a prime. The finite fields are generally called as *Galois fields* and denoted as **GF(P^n).**

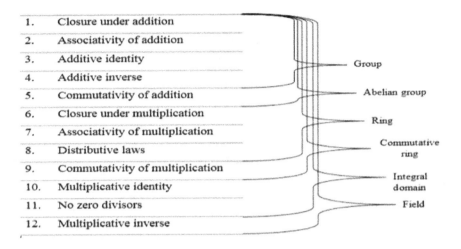

1.	Closure under addition
2.	Associativity of addition
3.	Additive identity
4.	Additive inverse
5.	Commutativity of addition
6.	Closure under multiplication
7.	Associativity of multiplication
8.	Distributive laws
9.	Commutativity of multiplication
10.	Multiplicative identity
11.	No zero divisors
12.	Multiplicative inverse

Group

Abelian group

Ring

Commutative ring

Integral domain

Field

Figure 4.6: Group, Ring, and Field

4.3.2 Modular Arithmetic

For a given positive integer n and for a non-negative integer a, if a is divided by n, we get an integer quotient q and a remainder r that obeys the following relationship:

$$a = qn + r \text{ where } 0 <= r < n \text{ and } q = \lfloor a/n \rfloor$$

$\lfloor z \rfloor$ is the largest integer less than or equal to z. Figure 4.6 illustrates that for a given "a" and positive "n", it is possible to find q and r that satisfy the preceding relationship.

Figure 4.7: Relation $a = qn + r$, where $0 <= r < n$

If a is an integer and n is a positive integer, we define *a mod n* (a modulo n) to be the remainder where a is divided by n. The integer n is called the **modulus**. Thus, for an integer a, we can write:

$a = \llcorner a/n \lrcorner * n + (a \bmod n)$

for example, $11 \bmod 7 = 4$ and $-11 \bmod 7 = 3$.

4.3.2.1   Modular Arithmetic Operations

The "mod q" operator maps all integers to the set of integers $\{0, 1, \ldots, (q\ 1)\}$. This raises a question if we can perform arithmetic operations within the confines of this set and this turns out that we can. This technique is called **modular arithmetic**. Modular arithmetic satisfies the following properties:

1. *{(a mod n) + (b mod n)} mod n = (a + b) mod n*
2. *{(a mod n) (b mod n)} mod n = (ab) mod n*
3. *{(a mod n) * (b mod n)} mod n = (a * b) mod n*

We demonstrate here the first property. Let's say *(a mod n) = r_a* and *(b mod n) = r_b*. Now, we can write $a = r_a + jn$ for integer j and $b = r_b + kn$ for integer k. Then

$(a + b) \bmod n = (r_a + jq + r_b + kn) \bmod n$

$= (r_a + r_b\ (k + j)\ n) \bmod n$

$= (r_a + r_b) \bmod n$

$= \{(a \bmod n) + (b \bmod n)\} \bmod n$

In the similar way remaining properties can also be proved.

4.3.2.2   Modular multiplicative inverse

In modular arithmetic, the **modular multiplicative inverse** of an integer a mod q is an integer x such that

$$a^{1} \equiv x \bmod n$$

It is a multiplicative inverse in the ring of integers modulo q denoted by Z_q. It is equivalent to

$$aa^{-1} \equiv ax \equiv 1\ (mod\ n)$$

The multiplicative inverse of *a mod n* exists if and only if *a* and *n* are co-prime (i.e., if gcd(*a*, *n*) = 1). If the modular multiplicative inverse of *a mod n* exists, the operation of division by *a* mod n can be defined as multiplying by the inverse, which is, in essence, the same concept as division in the field of real numbers.

4.3.2.3   Extended Euclidean algorithm

Extended Euclidean algorithm cab be used to find modular multiplicative inverse of *a modulo n*. The algorithm finds solutions to

$$ax + by = gcd(a,b)$$

where *a* and *b* are the given numbers and *x*, *y* and gcd(*a*, *b*) are the integer numbers that the algorithm determines. So, since the modular multiplicative inverse is the solution to

$$ax \equiv 1 \; mod \; n$$

by the definition of congruence, $n \mid (ax - 1)$, which means that n is a divisor of $ax - 1$. This, in turn, means

$$ax\text{-}1 = qn$$

Rearranging, we get

$$ax\text{-}qn = 1$$

where *a* and *n are* given, *x* is the inverse, and *q* is an integer multiple that will be discarded. Here, gcd(*a*, *n*) = 1 is predetermined.

4.3.2.4   Euler's theorem

Euler's theorem may be used as an alternative to the extended Euclidean algorithm to compute modular inverse: [50] According to Euler's theorem, if *a* is co-prime to *n*, i.e. gcd(*a*, *m*) = 1, then

$$a^{\varphi(m)} \equiv 1 \; mod \; n$$

where $\varphi(m)$ is Euler's totient function. This follows the fact that *a* belongs to the multiplicative group $(Z/nZ)^*$ iff *a* is co-prime to *n*. Therefore the modular multiplicative inverse can be found as:

$$a^{\varphi(m)-1} \equiv \alpha^{-1} \ mod \ n$$

if n is a **prime**, the modular inverse is given by:

$$\alpha^{-1} \equiv a^{n-2}(mod \ n)$$

4.4   Summary

The use of public key cryptography received considerable attention. An important advantage of chaos is that it is greatly sensitive to initial conditions and parameters and accurate duplication of it is impossible. Therefore, chaotic systems have more useful and practical applications. Cryptography and chaos have some common features, the most prominent being sensitivity to parameters' and variables' changes. The main attraction lies in a very unique property of chebyshev is that it is always restricted to the interval [-1 1]. This property can lead to implement novel cryptographic dynamic key generator.

Chapter 5

The proposed schemes

In this thesis, Two Chaos based signcryption schemes are purposed:

1. Multi messages single recipient and
2. Multi message multi recipient.

Both schemes provide unforgeability, confidentiality non-repudiation and integrity. A major improvement of the purposed schemes over H. Elkamchouchi's scheme [33] is public verification. The main idea, behind the purposed schemes, is to achieve high security by using chaos based dynamic structured key generator. The purposed signcryption scheme consists of four algorithm namely,

1. Key generation algorithm,
2. Multi Chaotic key generator,
3. Signcryption algorithm and
4. Unsigncryption algorithm.

Each user generates his private-public key pairs and should get the certificate for his public key from the certificate authority (CA) [2, 7, and 11]. The terms that are being used in our methodology, are given as:

p: a very large Prime Number

q: one of the large prime factor of p-1

g: a integer with order q mod p in $[1,...,p$-$1]$

5.1   Key Generation

The private and public keys of sender and receiver are generated in the following manner:

Pair of sender's key (x_a, y_a) is computed as follow:

x_a: Sender's private key chosen randomly from $[1,..., q$-$1]$

y_a: Sender's public key computed as:

$$y_a = g^{x_a} \bmod p$$

Pair of sender's keys (x_b, y_b) is computed as follow:

x_b: Receiver's private key chosen randomly from $[1,..., q\text{-}1]$

y_b: Receiver's public key computed as:

$$y_b = g^{x_b} \bmod p$$

5.2 Multi Chaotic Key Generator (MCKG)

The Multi Chaotic Keys Generator $MCKG(e, k_1, n)$ proposed here is three tuple, where e is generated using receiver's private key (x_b) and receiver's public key (y_b) or sender's public key (y_a), k_1 is digest of e and n is the total number of messages.

$$e = y_b^x \bmod p = (y_a \cdot g^{\sum_{i=1}^{n} r_i})^{s.x_b} \bmod p \text{ And } k_1 = hash(e) \qquad (1)$$

Suppose sender A wants to send n messages $(m_1, m_2, ..., m_n)$ to receiver B, he will generate n chaotic keys $(ckey_1, ckey_2, ..., ckey_n)$ for encryption as follow:

a) Represent k_1 as a number $k_1 \epsilon [-1, 1]$

b) $ckey_{i/2} = T_e(2. T_i^2(ckey_{i/2-1}) - 1)$ for i= 2,4..., 2.n $\qquad (2)$

Where $ckey_0 = k_1 \epsilon [-1 \ 1]$ $\qquad (3)$

The chaotic keys generated $(ckey_1, ckey_2, ..., ckey_n)$ by the MCKG is then used by the encryption and decryption algorithms.

5.3 Signcryption Schemes

This section defines two multi messages signcryption schemes. First scheme is defined for single recipient and the second is defines for multi recipient. In describing the schemes, we have used *hash* or H(.) to denote one way hash function, KH to denote keyed hash function, MCKG to denote multi chaotic key generator and (E, D) to denote symmetric key encryption and decryption algorithm.

5.3.1 Scheme I: Multi Message Single Recipient Signcryption Scheme

The Graphic representation of the scheme is shown in Figure 5.1. To signcrypt n messages, a user calculates n chaotic keys $(ckey_1, ckey_2, ..., ckey_n)$ used to encrypt the n messages $(m_1, m_2, ..., m_n)$ and then creates signature on n messages using his private key (x_b). n chaotic keys are generated using MCKG which takes 3 input e, k_1, and n.

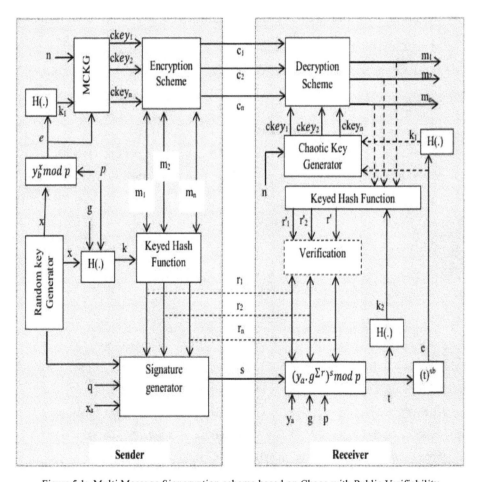

Figure 5.1: Multi Message Signcryption scheme based on Chaos with Public Verifiability

5.3.1.1 Signcryption algorithm

1. Calculate key $e = y_b^x \bmod p$ (4)
2. Calculate $k_1 = \text{hash}(e)$ (5)
3. Calculate $k_2 = \text{hash}(g^x \bmod p)$ (6)
4. Generate n chaotic keys using:

   $(ckey_1, ckey_2, \dots, ck_ney) = \text{MCKG}(e, k_1, n)$ (7)
5. Encrypt n messages using:

   $c_i = E_{ckey_i}(m_i)$ for $i = 1,\dots,n$ (8)
6. Calculate keyed hash values $(r_1, r_2,\dots, r_n)$ using k_2:

   $r_i = KH_{k2}(m_i)$ for $i = 1,\dots,n$ (9)
7. Generate signature using:

   $s = x(x_a + \sum_{i=1}^{n} r_i)^{-1} \bmod q$ (10)

   Sender sends signcrypted text (c_i, r_i, s) to receiver

On the receiver side, receiver can recover e, k_1 and k_2 successfully by using equations 11, 12, 13 and 14. Receiver then computes the chaotic keys to recover the messages.

Receiver then computes keyed hash values of decrypted messages under k_2 and comparing it to the received keyed hash values $((r_1, r_2, \dots, r_n)$ to check the integrity of the recovered messages. The unsigncryption algorithm is as follow:

5.3.1.2 Unsigncryption algorithm

1. Compute $t = (y_a \cdot g^{\sum_{i=1}^{n} r_i})^s \bmod p$ (11)
2. Compute $e = t^{xb} \bmod p$ (12)
3. Compute $k_1 = \text{hash}(e)$ (13)
4. Compute $k_2 = \text{hash}(t)$ (14)
5. For n messages compute n chaotic keys using

   $(ckey_1, ckey_2, \dots, ckey_n) = \text{MCKG}(e, k_1, n)$ (15)

6. Recover messages using

$$m_i = D_{ckey_i}(c_i) \text{ for } i = 1,...,n \tag{16}$$

7. Accept if $KH_{k1}(m_i) = r_i$ for $i = 1,...,n$ \hfill (17)

5.3.1.3 Correctness of the Purposed Scheme

Messages $(m_1, m_2, ..., m_n)$ can be recovered on receiver's side, if the signcrypted text is generated honestly by the sender, as the receiver B can recover the parameters e, k_1 by using his private key (x_b) and sender's public key (y_a) and can compute chaotic keys $(ckey_1, ckey_2, ..., ckey_n)$ which are used to decrypt the encrypted messages. j^{th} user can recover e^j and k_1^j by using (12) and (13), since

1) $e = t^{x_b} \bmod p$

$$= (y_a \cdot g^{\sum_{i=1}^n r_i})^{s \cdot x_b} \bmod p$$

$\quad$ Since, $t = (y_a \cdot g^{\sum_{i=1}^n r_i})^s \bmod p$

$$= (g^{x_a} \cdot g^{\sum_{i=1}^n r_i})^{s \cdot x_b} \bmod p$$

$$= (g^{x_a + \sum_{i=1}^n r_i})^{s \cdot x_b} \bmod p$$

$$= (g^{x_b \cdot (x_a + \sum_{i=1}^n r_i)})^s \bmod p$$

$$= (y_b)^{(x_a + \sum_{i=1}^n r_i) \cdot s} \bmod p$$

$$= (y^j)^x \bmod p$$

$\quad$ = value generated on sender's side

$\quad$ Since, $s = x(x_a + \sum_{i=1}^n r_i)^{-1} \bmod q$

2) $k_1 = hash(e^j)$

5.3.1.4 Nonrepudiation and public verifiability

If the sender A denies his signcrypted text, the receiver B_j can prove the dishonesty of the sender by sending data (m_i, r_i, s) for $i = 1,...,n$, to trusted third party (TTP) who can verify the origin of the message by calculating key k_2 using senders public key (y_a). TTP then calculate keyed hash values of messages and match them with received keyed hash values (r_i) to verify the origin of the messages. The TTP performs the following steps:

1. Calculate $k_2 = \text{hash}((y_a \cdot g^{\sum_{i=1}^{n} r_i})^s \bmod p)$
2. For $i=1$ to n
   a. Calculate $r'_i = KH_{k2}(m_i)$
   b. Check whether $r'_i = r_i$ to ensure if the origin of the messages is sender A.

During verification, confidentiality of the scheme is not affected, because the third party does not know sender's or receiver's private key to verify signature. Thus this purposed scheme provides public verifiability.

5.3.2 Scheme II: Multi Message Multi Recipient Signcryption Scheme

Let the total numbers of receivers be v. For a receiver B_j, his key pair is (x_b^j, y_b^j) for $j=1,...,v$ the sender calculates e^j using the jth user public key y_b^j and k_1^j using the one way hash function over e^j. He then computes n chaotic keys $(ckey_1^j, ckey_2^j, ..., ckey_n^j)$ to encrypt n messages $(m_1, m_2, ..., m_n)$ for the jth receiver. The sender then signs the n messages using his private key (x_a) and sends the signcrypted text to receiver j. The signcryption algorithm is as follow:

5.3.2.1   Signcryption algorithm

1. Calculate $e^j = (y_b^j)^x \bmod p$ (18)
2. Calculate $k_1^j = \text{hash}(e^j)$ (19)
3. Calculate $k_2 = \text{hash}(g^x \bmod p)$ (20)
4. for $i = 1,...,n$
   a. $c_i^j = E_{ckey_i^j}(m_i)$ (22)
   b. $r_i = KH_{k2}(m_i)$ (23)
5. $s = x(x_a + \sum_{i=1}^{n} r_i)^{-1} \bmod q$ (24)

Sender sends signcrypted text (c_i^j, r_i, s) to receiver j.

45

The jth receiver recovers the parameters e^j, k_1^j and k_2 (see (26), (27) and (28) respectively) using his private key (x_b^j) and sender's public key (y_a) and computes chaotic keys ($ckey_1^j$, $ckey_2^j$, ..., $ckey_n^j$) to decrypt the messages. After decrypting the messages, he then checks the integrity of the messages by computing keyed hash values of decrypted messages under k_2 and comparing it to the received keyed hash values (r_1, r_2, ..., r_n). The unsigncryption algorithm is as follow:

5.3.2.2   Unsigncryption algorithm

1. Calculate $t = (y_a \cdot g^{\sum_{i=1}^{n} r_i})^s \bmod p$ (25)

2. Calculate $e^j = t^{x_b^j} \bmod p$ (26)

3. Calculate $k_1^j = hash(e^j)$ (27)

4. Calculate $k2 = hash(t)$ (28)

5. For $i = 1,...,n$

    a. $ck_i^j = MCKG(e^j, k_1^j, n)$ (29)

    b. $m_i = D_{ckey_i^j}(c_i)$ (30)

    c.   Accept if $KH_{k2}(m_i) = r_i$ (31)

5.3.2.3   Correctness of the Purposed Scheme

Messages ($m_1, m_2, ..., m_n$) can be recovered on receiver's B_j side, for $j=1,...,v$, if the signcrypted text is generated honestly by the sender, as the jth receiver can recover the parameters e^j, k_1 by using his private key (x_b^j) and sender's public key (y_a) and can compute chaotic keys ($ckey_1, ckey_2, ..., ckey_n$) which are used to decrypt the encrypted messages. j^{th} user can recover e^j and k_1^j by using (26) and (27), since

1) $e^j = t^{x_b^j} \bmod p$

    $= (y_a \cdot g^{\sum_{i=1}^{n} r_i})^{s \cdot x_b^j} \bmod p$

    Since, $t = (y_a \cdot g^{\sum_{i=1}^{n} r_i})^s \bmod p$

$$= (g^{x_a} \cdot g^{\sum_{i=1}^n r_i})^{s \cdot x_b^j} \bmod p$$

$$= (g^{x_a + \sum_{i=1}^n r_i})^{s \cdot x_b^j} \bmod p$$

$$= (g^{x_b^j \cdot (x_a + \sum_{i=1}^n r_i)})^s \bmod p$$

$$= (y_b^j)^{(x_a + \sum_{i=1}^n r_i) \cdot s} \bmod p$$

$$= (y_b^j)^x \bmod p$$

$=$ value generated on sender's side

Since, $s = x(x_a + \sum_{i=1}^n r_i)^{-1} \bmod q$

2) $k_1^j = hash(e^j)$

5.3.2.4   Nonrepudiation and public verifiability

If the sender A denies his signcrypted text, the receiver B_j can prove the dishonesty of the sender by sending data (mi, ri, s) for $i = 1,\ldots,n$, to trusted third party (TTP) who can verify the origin of the message by calculating key k2 using senders public key (y_a). TTP then calculate keyed hash values of messages and match them with received keyed hash values (r_i) to verify the origin of the messages. The TTP performs the following steps:

1. Calculate $k_2 = hash((y_a \cdot g^{\sum_{i=1}^n r_i})^s \bmod p)$
2. For $i=1$ to n
   a. Calculate $r'_i = KH_{k2}(m_i)$
   b. Check whether $r'_i = r_i$ to ensure if the origin of the messages is sender A.

During verification, confidentiality of the scheme is not affected, since the third party does not know sender's or receiver's private key to verify signature. Thus this purposed scheme provides public verifiability.

5.4   Security features of purposed scheme

Table 5.1 compares the security features of different signcryption schemes. Security features of purposed schemes are described in the sub sections. The parameters on the bases of which different schemes are compared are confidentiality, integrity, unforgeability, public verification and chaos.

Table 5.1: Schemes comparison based on features provided

Scheme name	Confidentia-lity	Integrity	Unforgeabi-lity	Public Verification	Chaos based
Purposed Scheme I	YES	YES	YES	YES	YES
Purposed Scheme II	YES	YES	YES	YES	YES
Zheng	YES	YES	YES	NO	NO
M. Emarah, M. Elkamchouchi, A. Hagras	YES	YES	YES	NO	NO
M. Elkamchouchi	YES	YES	YES	NO	YES
Hassan Elkamchouchi, Mohammed Nasr, Roayat Ismail	YES	YES	YES	YES	NO

5.4.1 Confidentiality

To be secure, the information needs to be hidden from unauthorized access. To achieve this we must make the data non-intelligible, this is what confidentiality deals with. In the purposed schemes, if an attacker Eve wants to break the confidentiality he needs to know initial parameters to chaotic key generator. If he is able to find initial master key somehow, it is still infeasible for him to generate chaotic keys due to two reasons:

1) Use of one way hash function to generate master key,

2) Dynamic nature of chaotic key generator due to random polynomial generation. Therefore, it is quite infeasible for Eve to solve this.

5.4.2 Authenticity

In the both purposed schemes, the receiver and the judge can authenticate the sender's public key y_a with its certificate. Therefore the purposed schemes provide authentication of the message and the id of the sender.

5.4.3 Integrity

In our proposed schemes, the recipient can verify whether the received message is the original sent by the sender. In the signcryption phase, the sender computes and sends (C_i, r_i, s) to the recipient. If the attacker changes the cipher text C to C' then by the property of Random Oracle Model [7] it is infeasible for attacker to obtain the same digest for two different messages. [7]

5.4.4 Non-repudiation

The recipient should be able to prove to a third party that the sender has sent the signcrypted text. This ensures that the sender cannot deny his signcrypted texts. In the purposed schemes, if the sender A denies his signcrypted text, the receiver B_j can prove the dishonesty of the sender by sending data $\{(m_i, r_i, s)$ for $i = 1,...,n\}$ to trusted third party (TTP) who can verify the origin of the message by calculating key k_2 using senders public key (y_a). TTP then calculate keyed hash values of messages and match them with received keyed hash values (r_i) to verify the origin of the messages. The TTP performs the following steps:

1. Calculate $k_2 = \text{hash}((y_a \cdot g^{\sum_{i=1}^{n} r_i})^s \bmod p)$
2. Check whether $KH_{k2}(m_i) = r_i$ to ensure if the origin of the messages is sender A.

5.4.5 Public verifiability

Since the third party does not need sender's or receiver's private key to verify signature, confidentiality of the scheme is not affected. Thus the purposed scheme provides public verifiability.

5.5 Implementation of purposed scheme in c#

C# is an object oriented programming language which provides many inbuilt security features. In implementing purposed scheme, we have used .NET framework 4.0 which introduces a new variable *Biginteger* in C#. The main advantage of *Biginteger* is that it has no theoretical upper and lower limit. To handle decimal values new variable *Bigdecimal* is created in this implementation which makes use of *Biginteger* in its working. We have used MD5 hash function in implementation which gives 128 bits long digest value which is used as initial value to chaotic function.

To use hash value as initial value normalization is used which maps generated digest value the range [-1 1]. To normalize following formula is used:
Suppose we have a range from A-B and want to convert it to a scale of C to D then

$$k' = C+(k-A)*(D-C)/B-A$$

where k' is new value in the range C-D and k is in the range A-B. C# code for the normalization is given below:

decValue = BigInteger.Parse(k1, System.Globalization.NumberStyles.HexNumber);

range_low = BigInteger.Pow(2, 127);

range_high = (BigInteger.Pow(2, 127) - 1);

BigInteger total_range = range_high + range1_low;

BigDecimal total = new BigDecimal(total_range, 0);

BigDecimal two = new BigDecimal(2, 0);

BigDecimal bigDec = new BigDecimal(decValue, 0);

BigDecimal A = new BigDecimal(range1_low, 0);

k = (-total + (two * (bigDec + A))) / total;

Variable *k1* in the code above code is the master key generated after computing hash. The final value *k* is the normalized value which is in the range [-1 1]. The implemented scheme works for files a inputs and outputs. It uses AES cipher for encryption and decryption of files. Figure 5.2 to Figure 5.6 shows the snapshots of the implemented schemes.

Figure 5.2 shows the start form where files can be selected to signcrypt or unsigncrypt. In figure 5.3 five files are selected under the signcryption scheme. Figure 5.4 shows the generated parameters in signcryption.

In figure 5.5 and figure 5.6, unsigncryption scheme is shown. In figure 5.5, keyedHash files, signature file and encoded files are selected. Figure 5.6 shows the generated parameters in signcryption.

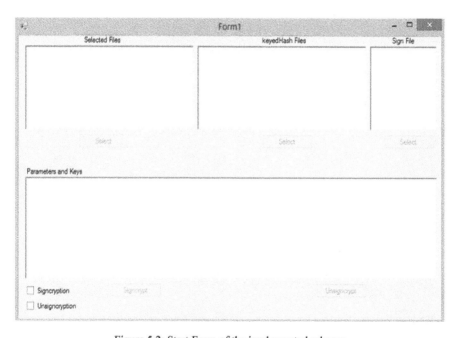

Figure 5.2: Start Form of the implemented scheme

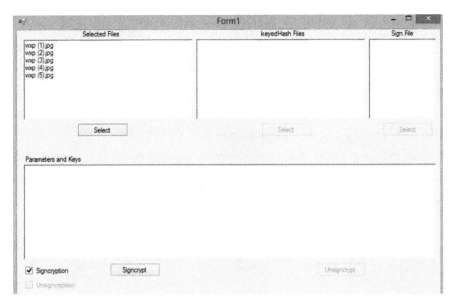

Figure 5.3: Files selected for signcryption phase

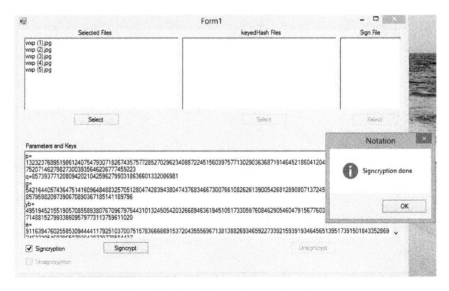

Figure 5.4: Completion of signcryption phase

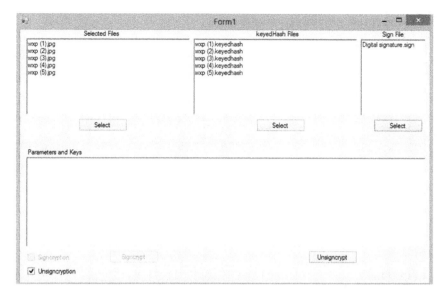

Figure 5.5: Files selected for signcryption phase

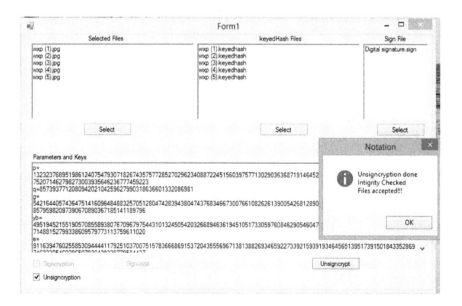

Figure 5.6: Completion of unsigncryption phase

5.6　Generated parameters and keys

This section shows the generated parameters and keys shown in the snap shots where "ch_i" represents the ith chaotic key generated. The generated parameters and keys are as follow:

p =
132323768951986124075479307182674357577285270296234088722451560397577
13029036368719146452186041204237350521785240337048752071462798273000
3935646236777459223

q = 8573937712080942021042596279903186366013320869811

g =
542164405743647514160964848832570512804742839438047437683466730076611
08262613900542681289080713724597310673074119355136085795982097390670
890367185141189796

Xa = 7926478533248359441252966752593161054517800620466

Ya =
107838279859368834078004788843768852580123291248165529944003186694177
12227984308664513720074342723253116776610426060680530302231490625440
3593803159583034340

Xb = 7742909844795631682061308285322071066855994961942

Yb =
495194521551905708558938076709679754431013245054203266894636194510511
73305976084629054604791567760329230977799786977904671488152799338609
579773113759611020

k1 = 6dba823346e338d0751839ce4d4c9b29

k2 = eb9d3d191e96352591439a4cf4be16a2

Ck1 =

16501670243188413444613414931141992209814217192731580914091671063065
98751353333983154584899795708164276195099992587232261361584535033454 8
234545615285352434E-154

Ck2 =

25565891254961986139518774818845996863666145453634287486915567479779
29311111843222945097762445811624944861543458011607287414803769761993
818335907474272933 E-154

Ck3 =

79077256951183558025119703267432856092594922618101292026819909832418
36059698718874229005565608933135970069922661356631938686454306731253
370147448673477073 E-154

Ck4 =

52502208552836128008405878521691644959730233854773972655128888956427
33763422903874235260719278578167669030379056209288408356988254742081
788677473325193114 E-154

Ck5 =

15920298115047752705601178223379481886159864928310492769195954739159
20264894503933079974567980552603460532208551119746578818115472804982
988976697984495203 E-154

The same keys are successfully recovered on the receiver's side (see section 5.3.1.1, 5.3.1.2 for the correctness).

5.7   Comparison to H. Elkamchouchi scheme

In Table 5.2 purposed schemes (PS) is compared with H. Elkamchouchi scheme (ES) in terms of total numbers of parameters in signcrypted text generated on sender's side. And saving is calculated with the following relation for 1 and 2 messages generated for up to four receivers.

$$Saving = \frac{Total\ parameters\ in\ ES - Total\ parameters\ in\ PS}{Total\ parameters\ in\ ES} * 100$$

Table 5.2: Saving in purposed scheme over H. Elkamchouchi scheme

Total Receivers \ Total messages	1	2
1	25.00%	00.00%
2	42.85%	12.50%
3	50.00%	18.18%
4	53.84%	21.42%

Chapter 6
Conclusion

In this thesis, two chaos based multi message signcryption schemes are proposed.

1. Multi Message Single Recipient Signcryption Scheme
2. Multi Message Single Recipient Signcryption Scheme

The main idea behind the purposed scheme is to develop a chaotic key generator which generates chaotic keys for encryption and decryption algorithm and to provide public verifiability. Multi chaotic key generator in the purposed scheme is dynamic in nature because the degree of polynomials is not fixed. Due to dynamic structure of chaotic key generator and chaotic nature of the keys, the purposed scheme provides very high security.

H. Elkamchouchi scheme discussed in chapter 3 is one of the most efficient chaos based signcryption scheme. However this scheme does not provide public verifiability. The purposed schemes achieve the public verifiability. This signifies that the signature of the sender can be verified publicly without the awareness of sender's or receiver's private key. In the purposed schemes, if there is only one receiver numerical value for the saving is 25% when one message is sent, if we increase the number of receivers and messages, numerical value for the saving reaches up to 53.84% and 21.42% for one and two messages generated for four users, over Elkamchouchi scheme[33].

6.1   Limitation of work

Chaos is sensitive to initial conditions. The multi chaotic key generator in the purposed scheme works in the range [-1 1]. For the practical implementation one needs to round off the generated number after some decimal places which may limit the sensitivity of the system to a particular number of digits of initial value.

6.2 Future work

However, the purposed schemes achieves public verifiability and numerical value for the saving of 53.84% and 21.42% for one and two messages sent to four users, over Elkamchouchi, large degree of polynomial may affect the efficiency of the system in some cases in comparison to non-chaotic signcryption schemes. Now we should look forward to implement a new chaotic key generator which is dynamic in nature and efficient than that of the purposed one.

References

[1] Y. Zheng, "Digital Signcryption or How to Achieve Cost (Signature & Encryption) << Cost (Signature) + Cost (Encryption)," Advances in Cryptology - Crypto'97, LNCS 1294, Springer, pp. 165-179, 1997.

[2] William Stallings. Cryptography and Network security: Principles and Practices. Prentice Hall Inc., fifth edition, 2011.

[3] Claude E. Shannon, "Communication theory of secrecy systems," Bell System Technical Journal, pp. 656-715,http://www.cs.ucla.edu/jkong/research/security/shannon.html

[4] Whitfield Diffie and Martin E. Hellmann "New directions in cryptography," IEEE Transactions on Information Theory, IT -22(6):644–654, November 1976

[5] Bruce Schneier, Applied Cryptography: Protocols, Algorithms, and Source Code in C. John Wiley & Sons, Inc., second edition, 1996

[6] Paul C. van Oorschot, Alfred J. Menezes and Scott A. Vanstone, Handbook of Applied Cryptography, CRC Press, 1996.

[7] Behrouz A. Forouzan, Cryptography and Network Security, Tata McGraw-Hill, 2007.

[8] Varad Kirtane and C, Pandu Rangan, Rsa-tbos, "Signcryption with proxy reencryption," In DRM '08: Proceedings of the 8th ACM workshop on Digital rights, 2008 management, pages 59-66, New York, NY, USA, 2008. ACM.

[9] Yuliang Zheng, Joonsang Baek, Ron Steinfeld "Formal proofs for the security of signcryption," Journal of Cryptology, 20(2):203-235, 2007.

[10] William J Caelli, Edward P Dawson, and Scott A Rea. Pki, "Elliptic curve cryptography, and digital signatures," Computers and Security, 18(1):47 - 66, 1999.

[11] Lawrence C, Washington, Elliptic Curves: Number Theory and Cryptography. CRC Press, 2003.

[12] Surya A. Effendi R, Sutikno, "An implementation of ElGamal elliptic curves cryptosystems," pages 483-486, Nov 1998

[13] Ren-Junn Hwang, Chih-Hua Lai, and Feng-Fu Su, "An efficient signcryption scheme with forward secrecy based on elliptic curve," Applied Mathematics and Computation, 167(2):870 - 881, 2005.

[14] M. Elkamchouchi, A-A. M. Emarah Esam A. A. Hagras: "Public Key Multi-Message Signcryption (PK-MMS) Scheme For Secure Communication Systems," Fifth Annual Conference on Communication Networks and Services Research(CNSR), 2007

[15] Benoit Libert, J- J. Quisquater: "A new identity based signcryption scheme from pairing," IW2003, Paris, France, paper 11.3.4, p. 109, March 31 -April 4, 2003.

[16] Y. Zheng, H. Imai, "How to construct efficient Signcryption Schemes on elliptic curves," Proc. of IFIP/SEC'98, Chapman & Hall, 1998

[17] Yuliang Zheng, "Efficient Signcryption Schemes on Elliptic Curves," Advances in cryptology, Vol. 10, pp. 15-19, 2000.

[18] Y. Zheng, "Signcryption and its applications in efficient public key solutions," Proceeding of ISw97, pp. 291-312,1998.

[19] Yuliang Zheng, Alexander W. Dent, Moti Yung, Practical Signcryption, 2010

[20] National Institute of Standards and Technology (NIST), NIST FIPS PUB 186-3 – Digital Signature Standard (DSS), 2009. Available from http://csrc.nist.gov/publications/PubsFIPS.html.

[21] C. P. Schnorr, "Efficient signature generation for smart cards" In G. Brassard, editor, Advances in Cryptology – Crypto '89, volume 435 of Lecture Notes in Computer Science, pages 239–252. Springer, 1989.

[22] M. Toorani, A. Beheshti, "Cryptanalysis of an Elliptic Curve-based Signcryption Scheme," International Journal of Network Security, Vol.10, No.1, PP.51-56, Jan 2010.

[23] J. Baek, R. Steinfeld, and Y. Zheng, "Formal proofs for the security of signcryption," In D. Naccache and P. Paillier, editors, Public Key Cryptography, volume 2274 of Lecture Notes in Computer Science, pages 80–98. Springer, 2002.

[24] X. Yang Y. Han and Y. Hu, "Signcryption based on elliptic curve and its multi-party schemes," Proceedings of the 3rd ACM International Conference on Information Security (InfoSecu 04), pages 216-217, 2004.

[25] Mohsen Toorani and Ali Asghar Beheshti Shirazi, "Cryptanalysis of an efficient signcryption scheme with forward secrecy based on elliptic curve," Computer and Electrical Engineering, International Conference on, pp. 428-432, 2008.

[26] R.H. Deng, F. Bao, "A signcryption scheme with signature directly verifiable by public key," Proceedings of PKC'98 LNCS 1431, pages 55-59, 1998.

[27] Ana Gamage, Jussipekka Leiwo, and Yuliang Zheng. "Encrypted message authentication by firewalls," In Proc. of PKC99, LNCS 1560, pages 69-81, Springer-Verlag, 1999.

[28] Yiliang Han, Xiaolin Gui, "Multi-recipient Signcryption for Secure Group Communication," Industrial Electronics and Applications, 2009 ICIEA 2009. 4th IEEE conference on, pp. 161-164, 25-27 May 2009

[29] Fateman, R.J, "Lookup tables, recurrences, and complexity," In Proc. Int. Symp. Sym-bolic and Algebraic Computation. ISSAC, pp. 68–73, 1989

[30] H. Elkamchouchi, Mohammed Nasr, and R. Ismail, "A New Efficient Multiple Messages Signcryption Scheme with Public Verifiability," L. Qi (Ed.): FCC 2009, CCIS 34, pp. 193–200, 2009.

[31] Xuanwu Zhou, "Improved Signcryption Scheme with Public Verifiability," Knowledge Engineering and Software Engineering, (KESE '09) Pacific Asia Conference on, pp. 178-181, 19-20 Dec, 2009

[32] Ranjan Bose and Amitabh Banerjee, "Implementing symmetric cryptography using chaos functions," 7th Int. Conf. On Advanced Computing and Communications Dec 20-22, Roorkee, India, 1999

[33] Dalia H. Elkamchouchi: "A Chaotic Public Key Multi-Message Multi-Recipients Signcryption Scheme (CPK-MM-MR-SS)," 12th World Multi-Conference on Systemics, Cybernetics and Informatics: (WMSCI), 2008

[34] Lorenz attractor. D. V. Anosov (originator), Encyclopedia of Mathematics. URL: http://www.encyclopediaofmath.org/index.php?title=Lorenz_attractor&oldid=123 39

[35] Kellert, Stephen H., In the Wake of Chaos: Unpredictable Order in Dynamical Systems, University of Chicago Press, 1993

[36] Danforth, Christopher, "Chaos in an Atmosphere Hanging on a Wall", Mathematics of Planet Earth, April 2013.

[37] Hasselblatt, Boris, Anatole Katok, A First Course in Dynamics: With a Panorama of Recent Developments. Cambridge University Press, 2003, ISBN 0-521-58750-6.

[38] Fagen Li, Masaaki Shirase, and Tsuyoshi Takagi, "Identity-Based Hybrid Signcryption," International Conference on Availability, Reliability and Security, pp. 534-539, 2012

[39] Elaydi, Saber N., Discrete Chaos. Chapman & Hall/CRC, p. 117, 1997.

[40] Basener, William F. Topology and its applications, Wiley. p. 42, 2006

[41] LIU Pei-yu, XUE Wen-juan, "A Signcryption Scheme with Message Link Recovery," International Symposium on Information Technology in Medicine And Education, 2012

[42] Devaney, Robert L., An Introduction to Chaotic Dynamical Systems, second edition, Westview Press, 2003

[43] Fateman, R.J, "Lookup tables, recurrences, and complexity," In Proc. Int. Symp. Sym-bolic and Algebraic Computation. ISSAC, pp. 68–73, 1989

[44] Alligood, K.T.; Sauer, T.; Yorke, J.A, "Chaos: an introduction to dynamical systems," Springer-Verlag, 1997

[45] Richard Culham, Chebyshev polynomials, March 2004. Available from: http://www.mhtl.uwaterloo.ca/courses/me755/web_chap6.pdf

[46] Xuanwu Zhou, "Improved Signcryption Scheme with Public Verifiability," Knowledge Engineering and Software Engineering (KESE '09), Pacific Asia Conference on,pp. 178-181, 19-20 Dec. 2009

[47] LjupcoKocarev , ShiguoLian (Eds.), Chaos-Based Cryptography, Springer, chapter 2, 2011

[48] Jacobson, Nathan, Basic algebra 1, second edition, Dover, 2009.

[49] J. J. O'Connor and E. F. Robertson, "The development of Ring Theory," September 2004

[50] Thomas Koshy, Elementary number theory with applications, 2nd edition, ISBN 978-0-12-372487-8.P. 346.

Appendix A

Fast computation of the Product of Multiple exponentials

In unsigncryption, , $a_0^{b_0} a_1^{b_1}$ mod p is one of the most expensive part of computation where a_0, a_1, b_0, b_1 and p are large prime numbers. According to A. Shamir, the product involving the same modulo can be obtained with a less computational cost by applying the following algorithm:

INPUTS:

Group elements $g_0, g_1, \dots, g_{k-1}$ and non-negative m-bit integers $b_0, b_1, \dots, b_{k-1}$.

OUTPUTS: $g_0^{b_0} g_1^{b_1} \dots g_{k-1}^{b_{k-1}}$

ALGORITHM:
1. *Precomputation*

   For $i=0$ to $(2^k - 1)$: $G_i \leftarrow \prod_{j=0}^{k-1} g_j^{i_j}$ where $i = (i_{k-1} \dots i_0)_2$
2. $A \leftarrow 1$.
3. For i form 1 to t do the following $A \leftarrow A. A, A \leftarrow A. G_{I_i}$
4. Return(A)